Buckskin & Buffalo

Buckskin & Buffalo

The Artistry of the Plains Indians

Colin F. Taylor

RIZZOLI
NEW YORK

First published in the United States of America
in 1998 by
RIZZOLI INTERNATIONAL PUBLICATIONS, INC.
300 Park Avenue South, New York, NY 10010

First published in Great Britain in 1998 by
Salamander Books Ltd
8 Blenheim Court
Brewery Road
London N7 9NT

ISBN 0-8478-2087-4
LC 97-75704

EDITOR
Chris Westhorp
DESIGNER
Mark Holt
FILMSET
SX DTP, England
REPRODUCTION
Emirates Printing Press
Printed in Singapore

For Joseph:
George P. Horse Capture's
"Whirlwind Soldier"

Contents

Introduction

Kicking Bear, Miniconjou

Buffalo/Bison
(Bison americanus)
Pronghorn/Antelope
(Antilicapra americana)
Elk/Wapiti
(Cervus canadensis)
Bighorn
(Ovis canadensis)

In the early 1860s an Indian agent in the Upper Missouri River region made an observation of the Plains Indians: "powerful and warlike people, proud, haughty and defiant – well over six feet in height, strong muscular frames and very good horsemen, well dressed, principally in skins and robes, rich in horses and lodges, have a great abundance of meat since buffalo, elk, antelope and deer abound in their country. They say they are Indians and do not wish to change their mode of living."[1]

Remarks were also made about the non-human inhabitants of the region:

"Of all the quadrupeds that have lived upon the earth, probably no other species ever marshaled such innumerable hosts as those of the American bison. It would have been as easy to count or estimate the number of leaves in a forest as to calculate the number of buffaloes living at any given time during the history of the species previous to 1870."[2]

On the day that Lieutenant Colonel Phil Sheridan, commander of the U.S. Army's Department of the Southwest, brazenly encouraged the "festive cowboy" to populate the Plains with "speckled cattle," he was sounding the death knell of the Plains Indians. What he was encouraging, and what apparently needed little goading, was the wholesale destruction of *Bison americanus* at the hands of buffalo hunters, freelancers and employees of the railroad companies, with their fifty-calibre Sharps buffalo rifles.

In the early 1870s, William Blackmore, an English traveller, reported that buffalo were being slaughtered purely for their hides at the rate of one million per annum. Professional hunters formed lines of camps along the Arkansas River and continuously shot buffalo night and day as they came down to drink.

The heart of the very heartland of the great Plains, home to the Blackfeet, Arapaho, Cheyenne, Sioux, Crow, Hidatsa, Comanche and Kiowa, was torn out by the arrival of the white man. The old free life of the Indian was swept away – the buffalo was slaughtered to near extinction; the established pat-

American Horse, Oglala

terns of inter-tribal trade were broken; religious, ceremonial and social organizations were destroyed; the systems of values by which the Plains Indians had interpreted and organized their lives were done away with.

This book, however, is not a polemic regarding historical injustice and the plight of the North American Indian today. Its theme is somewhat simpler, if equally poignant. It focusses on the material culture of the Plains Indians – how they lived off the land and how the creatures that fed off it became an art form.

The Plains Indians developed a distinctive way of life. The horse was vital to their culture. They were nomadic hunters, hunting game – pronghorn and elk for example – and following the buffalo herds. The buffalo was essential to their very existence for it supplied the basis of all their needs, from clothing and food to cooking utensils, weapons, ornaments and tools. So much did their lifestyle pivot around the existence of buffalo and game and their abil-

Medicine Crow, Crow

ity to hunt them both freely and without any restrictions, that with the destruction of the immense buffalo herds by the end of the nineteenth century, the Plains Indians' traditional way of life came to an end.

What ended too was a particular form of "material culture" which had derived from the creatures they hunted. The Plains Indians were herded now onto reservations and away from their traditional hunting grounds, and could no longer pursue their old nomadic way of life; those who had cre-

ated an everyday art form had to adjust to a new way of life.

Luckily, not everything was lost; while much of the Plains Indians' material culture was wantonly destroyed in the greed to acquire land, a small and precious part had been acquired over time by ethnologists and interested individuals and remains today in the collections of European and North American museums. It constitutes an extraordinary legacy which offers a remarkable insight into the way a particular group of people lived during the last century.

Buckskin and buffalo hide were integral to the way of life of the Plains Indians; they lived off the animals in every sense. This book celebrates some of the exquisite items the Plains tribes produced. Adorned also with the skin and bone of other creatures, these pieces are drily called artifacts in the museum collections, but a better description would be "silent memorials" since they are redolent of a particular and precious way of life, one of living purely off the land – and one that today has all but disappeared into the bleak Plains.

Thus, the purpose of this book is straightforward: to illustrate simply and beautifully some of the more exquisite items of the Plains Indians' culture which were derived from the deer or buffalo. These range from women's dresses, children's clothes and men's ceremonial or "war" shirts to shields, buffalo robes and parfleches. Each piece has its own, very apparent aesthetic; each one has variety, pattern and vitality and reflects the particular traits of the tribe that

Two Comanche girls

produced it. Additionally, the construction of each item is examined in terms of decoration and style of adornment, highlighting the use of porcupine quills and beads, eagle, hawk or crow feathers and the use of particular colors. A number of these items are replete with symbolism – much of it specific to the individual owner of the object – and the text attempts to reveal some of their more arcane details.

Buckskin & Buffalo is therefore a respectful tribute to the dynamic, resilient and highly resourceful Plains people who produced these magnificent "silent memorials" which speak to us still.

Notes

1 Samuel N. Latta, Indian Agent, Upper Missouri, circa 1860.

2 Hornaday, 1887: Part II: p.373.

This Kiowa painting on deerskin, exceptional for its exquisite colors and realism, was collected by the ethnologist James Mooney in 1891. It depicts an episode in the Sun Dance which was generally celebrated annually during the third week of June. Part of the ceremonial involved the procession of the women to cut down a selected tree to be used as the central pole within the medicine lodge. Shown here is the tree with the warriors return-ing to the women to inform them of its location. Shown at lower right, a tribute with a pipe is made to a painted shrine, which is supported on a pole frame. This rawhide shrine, with its boat-like shape, contains the sacred *Taime* of the Kiowa, an icon which originated among the Crow and which was held in great awe by tribal mem-bers: it was central to the correct performance of the Sun Dance ceremonials.

Mandan Robe

A buffalo robe documenting the exploits of *Mato-tope*, or Four Bears, a well-known second chief of the Mandan who, in 1834 when this robe was collected, lived in the earth lodge of *Mih-Tutta-Hang-Kush*, adjacent to which stood the trading post of Fort Clark on the Missouri River. The pictographic techniques which he developed are distinctive for their realism. An outstanding warrior, Four Bears was involved in at least twelve battles in which he took a total of fourteen scalps. Several of these episodes are depicted on the robe, including one dramatic exploit when he was badly wounded in the hand in a great battle with a Cheyenne (lower right). The robe is further embellished with a band of dyed porcupine quillwork in yellow, red, blue and brown. The hair-locks on the edge probably refer to coups counted in battle and horses captured or given away.

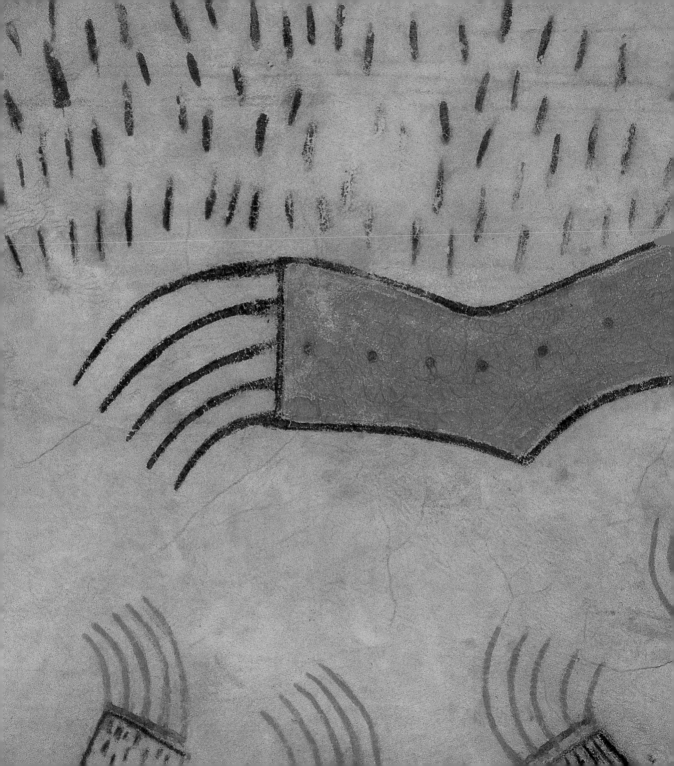

Crow Shield

A Crow buckskin shield cover, circa 1840. These were generally laced over a heavy buffalo rawhide disc some 20 inches (50cm) in diameter. Several covers, each painted differently, could be associated with a particular shield. The designs, which were exposed to the enemy in battle, were believed to evoke supernatural powers that would protect and aid the owner. The mechanical protection afforded by the rawhide was of secondary importance. Recognizing the great courage, strength and ferocity of the grizzly bear, ambitious warriors sought – by visions or dreams – to acquire some of its power, invoking protection by the painted symbols. Dominant here is a grizzly bear paw to ward off enemy fire, illustrating the bear's ability to protect its young, as represented by the smaller paws shown on the lower part of the shield.

A heavily beaded and hair-fringed shirt (back view) made more than a century ago and collected from the Omaha by Francis La Flesche, a member of the tribe, in the late nineteenth century. Such garments are relatively rare because they were worn only by individuals who held high status within the tribe. In this case the owner was endowed with the coveted bear power (see pages 14–15), and the shirt's designs refer to images seen by him in a vision. This magnificent and colorful garment represents the authority of the supernatural, a force which was symbolized in rituals confirming the office of high-ranking individuals. It is heavily fringed with human hairlocks, each one bound with sinew and painted blue-green. The crescent-shaped neck flap is unusual – on most Plains shirts it is triangular or rectangular.

This Arapaho boy's shirt illustrates the heavy tanned buckskin which was often used to fabricate garments – shirts, leggings, dresses – on the Southern Plains. The hides were generally from deer or mountain sheep, the prime hides obtained from animals hunted in the early winter. After a laborious tanning technique utilizing a mixture of brains and liver, the result was not only waterproof but often as soft as velvet. A degree of tailoring is in evidence, and is characteristic of Southern Plains clothing. Dating from circa 1890, this shirt's main decoration is the fringing that runs from the shoulders and along the edges of the neck flap, together with the lane seed beadwork in white and blue. The eagle feather is flanked by red and black flicker feathers and the pendants were described at the time of collection – probably by the owner – as "sacred medicine."

Blackfeet Robe

This rare and beautifully dressed elk-skin robe was collected by Count d'Otrante at Fort McKenzie in the heart of Blackfeet territory in 1843. This has been identified as part of the regalia worn by the Holy Woman who both initiated and led the Blackfeet Sun Dance ceremonials. The main painted motifs consist of Maltese Star–like patterns in green and red, which at a glance appear identical. In fact, those in green represent *apunni,* the moth or butterfly, while those in red are the Morning Star, considered by the Blackfeet to be the son of the Moon and Sun and a great source of protective power. The red conveys the condition of being saturated with Sun power. This unusual combination is explained in Blackfeet mythology, which is replete with references to flying insects which acted as sacred messengers between the sky powers and earth-bound man.

This dress, dating from circa 1870, was collected by the agent to the Nez Perce, J. B. Monteith. It shows many of the characteristics typical of the work of this Plateau tribe, a number of whom traveled and lived with the Crow Indians of western Montana. Made of two whole skins – probably bighorn – the ample skirt well suited the needs of equestrian nomads. The straight cut of the lower edge of the skirt, and the emphasis on undula-tions in the beadwork across the cape, with the lanes curving up to join those on the other side, underline the differences between dresses of the Plateau tribes and those of the true Plains people. Without analysis of this type, it would be easy to suggest that this is of Blackfeet (Plains) origin, since both tribes continued using the large pony beads on women's dresses long after they had gone out of fashion with most other tribes.

Magnificent dresses such as this one were popular among the Lakota after about 1870, when seed beadwork flourished among most of the Plains tribes. Dresses from the Northern and Central Plains were traditionally made of two deerskins and were often referred to as "deer tail" dresses, since the tail of the deer was on the chest and back of the wearer (see pages 22–23). In this example, circa 1880, the deer tail embellishment has been replaced with a symbolic U-shaped design in beadwork; Lakota women used it to represent a turtle, since turtles were considered to have power over fertility and the period of infancy. Likewise, the two beaded diamonds flanked by triangles on the left and right sides of the cape may well refer to buffalo power – the buffalo, like woman, was considered to give "continuity of existence."

Southern Cheyenne Dress

This is a typical dress from the Southern Plains region, in a style that was particularly popular from about 1880 onwards. It almost certainly evolved from the separate cape and skirt which were widely used in Mexico and beyond. It contrasted with the deer tail dress (see pages 22–23) in that it was constructed of three deerskins. In this illustration, the contours of the animal hide – front and back legs – can be discerned easily. Dec-oration is in the form of more than two hundred coveted elk teeth, much valued items, since each creature yielded only two that were suitable for such embellishments. Narrow lanes of beadwork across the body and lower part of the dress, together with red paint, tin cone jingles and heavy fringing, complete this magnificent garment, which was collected by the ethnologist James Mooney in 1890.

A quilled shirt collected from the Upper Missouri region, probably dating from about 1840. While some trimming is evident on the arms of this garment, the lower body contours, with the legs intact, clearly show that it has been fabricated in the traditional way from two skins – possibly antelope since the hide is unusually thin. Embelishments are in the form of bands and rosettes of porcupine quillwork with fringes of horse and human hair. The garment is also elaborately painted with pictographic motifs showing not only warriors in combat but also details of war accoutrements such as bows and arrows, quivers, a shield, guns and warbonnets. The geometrical motifs on the lower part of the shirt probably refer to horses captured. The distinctive style of pictographic paintings suggests that this is of Gros Ventre origin.

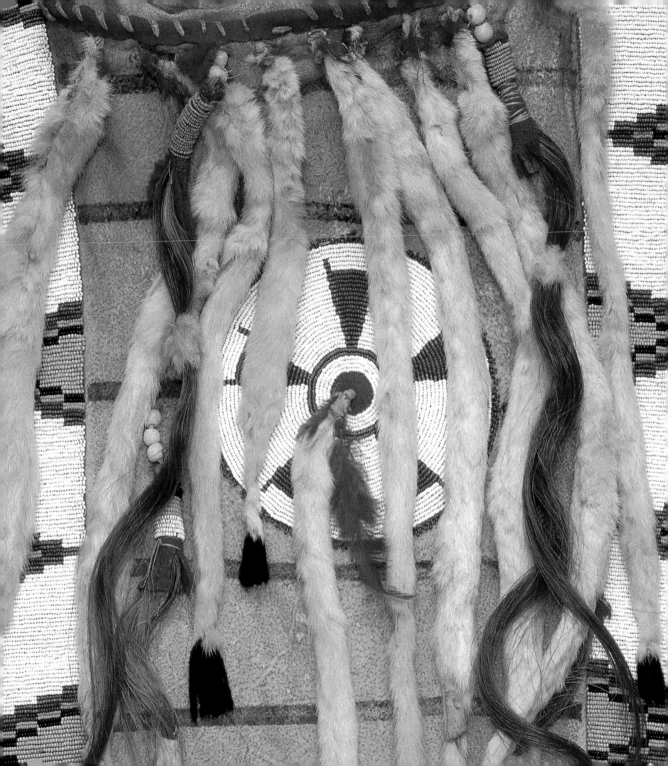

Piegan Shirt

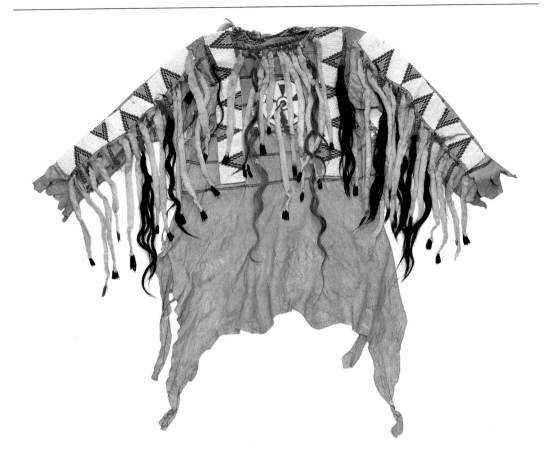

Although this shirt was collected from the Piegan in 1903, it is of a style popular a generation earlier. The Piegan were the most southerly of the three Blackfeet tribes residing during the historic period, mainly in the region that is now northern Montana. Triangular motifs as shown on this shirt (back view, allowing the decorative features to be seen more clearly) were particularly favored by the Blackfeet and appear in the porcupine quillwork which predated beadwork. The beaded bands are worked in the so-called overlaid stitch and are combined with ermine and hair fringing. While the ermine is highly decorative, it came from the weasel, an animal recognized for its tenacity and fearlessness, attributes desired by all Plains warriors. The idea of using discs (top, center) was probably introduced to the Blackfeet by the Assiniboin in the early nineteenth century.

Sioux Dress

This dress from the Sioux at Fort Peck breaks with tradition in that the entire garment is fully beaded instead of just the cape (see pages 24–25). The style illustrates an extension of the artwork that commenced in the late nineteenth century when large amounts and extensive areas of beadwork were being produced by Sioux women. This is a particularly fine example, and well documented. The dress was made by a Mrs. Minnie Sky Arrow,

an accomplished pianist who wore this as a recital gown. While most of the beadwork is in the so-called lazy stitch, which is typical of the Sioux, some – at the edges of the skirt – is in the overlaid technique, which probably shows Assiniboin influence. The dress is heavily fringed with buckskin and the tin cone jingles on the bottom side extensions would make a pleasant sound when the wearer was moving.

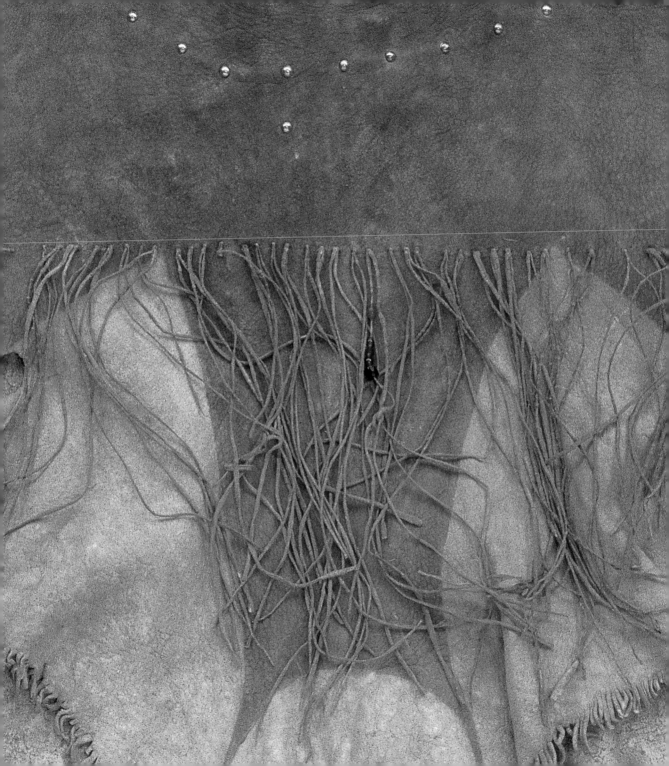

Comanche Garment

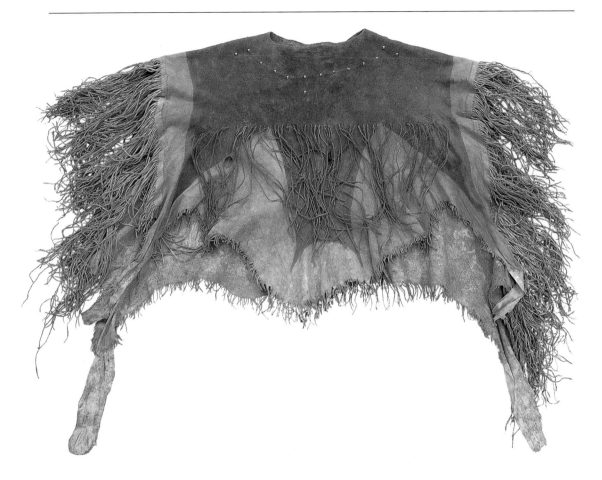

This Comanche woman's cape was collected about 1840 by the explorer and botanist Jean Louis Berlandier. It is made of one complete deerskin folded in half. Although constructed in a simple manner, it is elegantly embellished with a red painted design, which itself follows the contour of the hide. That trade contacts were present is indicated by the use of small metal buttons around the neck and glass beads pendant at the center of the chest. The twisted fringes typical of Southern Plains leatherwork are laced into the body of the cape and painted red, adding further embellishment. Such capes were generally worn with a buckskin apron, a combination similar to that of the Indians of Mexico, as described by Spanish explorers in the sixteenth century. This probably led to the development of the three-skin dress, which became so popular later (see pages 26–27).

This fully beaded pair of Crow boy's moccasins was collected in Montana by the ethnologist W. J. Hoffman in 1892. Early examples of Crow moccasins were made from one piece of heavy buckskin described by one observer as "in the manner of mittens." This style remained popular well into the second half of the nineteenth century, when it was replaced by the hard-sole moccasin which, as shown here, had uppers of heavy tanned hide sewn to soles of rawhide with sinew thread. The overlaid stitch, and the colors and patterns are typical of Crow beadwork of this period. The main decorative motifs are the U-shaped designs on the vamps, which represent horsetracks and indicate horses captured from the enemy. In this case they probably document the achievements of the boy's older brother or his father, decorations of this sort being highly subjective.

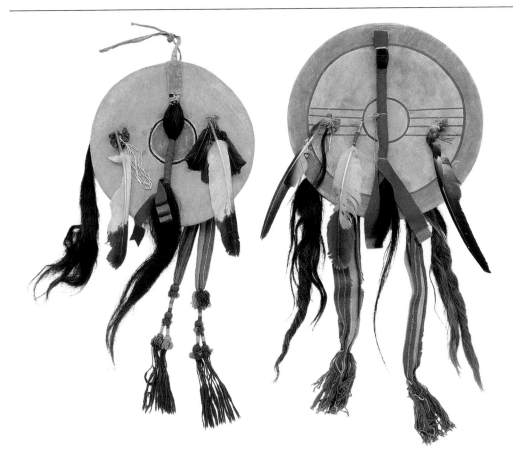

Two model shields which were made for and col-lected by the ethnologist James Mooney as speci-mens for part of a project relating to Kiowa her-aldry, begun circa 1890. The shield design shown in detail on the left belonged to *Padalti*, or Fur Man, grandson of *Dohasan*, who was head chief of the Kiowas until his death in 1866. The shield at the right was made to the specification of *Tsonkiada*, who was the original owner of the design (such designs could be traded). The central painted disc of each shield represents a buffalo wallow (a mark on the ground made when a buf-falo rolls in the dust); each has cloth and buffalo hair pendants, with decorative red cloth wraps displaying distinctive selvedge. Each is also embellished with feathers of the golden eagle (left, brown tipped) and the hawk (right) – sym-bols of courage, determination, speed and power.

This fine shield, which displays much military and religious symbolism, was captured by General Henry Lawton in 1876. It was identified as formerly in the possession of the Oglala war chief Crazy Horse. It is made of a large disc of buffalo rawhide some 20 inches (50cm) in diameter, over which is carefully laced a heavy soft-tanned buckskin cover. The general layout of the shield design and the rendering of the stars conforms to those traditionally used by the Lakota, although the "man power symbol" (the bifurcated red and black figure on the left) and the long red breech-cloth suggest a Cheyenne influence. The large bear above the central disc probably refers to the owner's spiritual guardian, while the Thunderbird and lightning motifs relate to communication with the higher powers. There is clearly reference here to confrontation between different cultures.

40

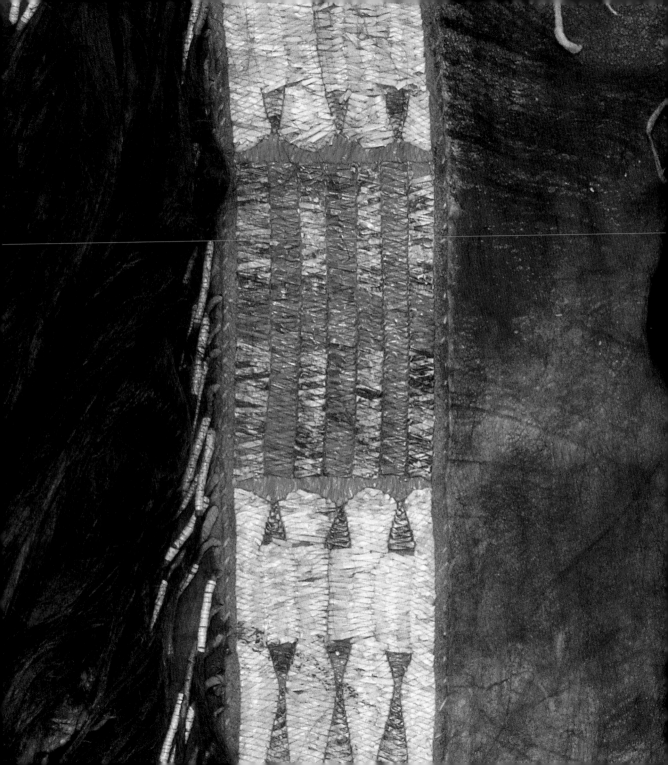

Cheyenne Shirt

A Cheyenne human-hair-fringed shirt of tanned antelope hide, which formerly belonged to Little Chief – possibly the same man who visited Washington DC in 1850. The decoration consists of broad bands of porcupine quillwork over the shoulders and down the arms, using a variant of the so-called "plaited" technique. At the throat and back are narrow triangular flaps which consist of buckskin covered with blue and red cloth deco-rated with beadwork and embellished at the edges with human hair-locks. The upper part of the shirt is painted with dark blue earth paint, the lower part with yellow. Such painting is highly symbolic, representing sky and earth powers: the blue paint, for example, was traditionally derived from a formation produced by a lightning strike. This is a back view; the hair fringes would be on the outer edges of the arms when worn.

Cheyenne Shirt

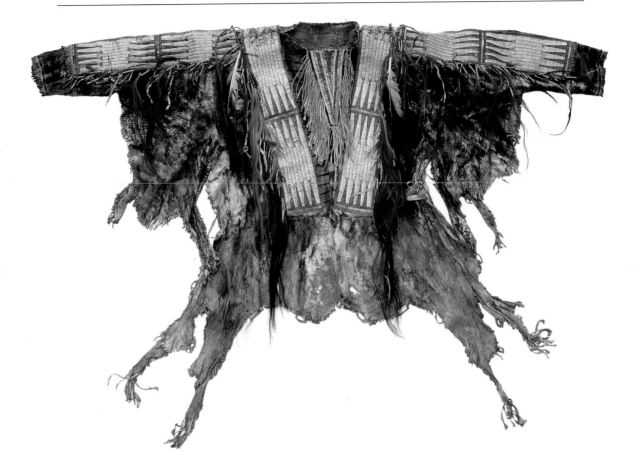

An early, magnificently embellished Cheyenne shirt, which probably dates from about 1870. This has been fabricated from two complete deer or antelope hides, the top one-third of the hide producing the arms, the lower two-thirds forming the body of the shirt. Note that the skin from both front and back legs of the animal can be seen under the arms and at the bottom of the shirt. Such completeness allowed identification with the spirit of the animal, and traditionally male animal hides would be used for men's garments of this type. Cheyenne mythology attributes the origin of such sacred garments to their prophet-hero, Sweet Medicine. In addition to the broad bands of porcupine quillwork across the shoulders and down the arms, there is heavy embellishment mainly of locks of horsehair, which probably refer to horses captured in war.

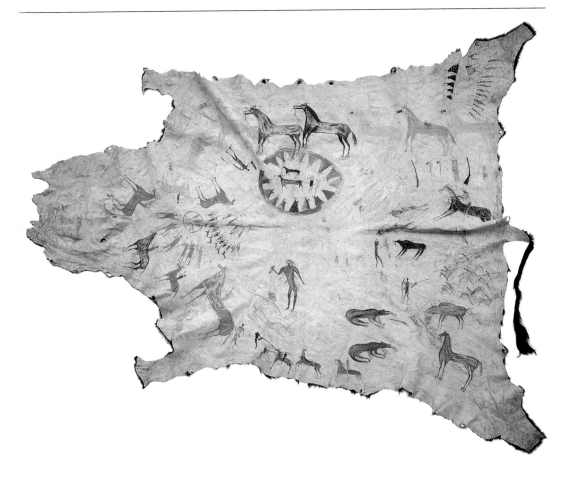

A large tanned steer hide painted in the spring of 1892 by the Piegan artist Sharp. This was collected by the physician Dr. Z. T. Daniel on the Blackfeet Reservation in Montana, together with a detailed explanation of the actions portrayed. The pictographs, in a style typical of the Blackfeet of this period, mainly document the military exploits of White Grass, a highly respected chief of the Buffalo Chip band of the Piegan, who was involved in many actions against such tribes as the Flathead and Pend d'Oreilles of the Plateau region to the west of Blackfeet territory. Here, White Grass is about to enter the Flathead circle of tipis to cut free the two valuable picketed horses at the very heart of the encampment. He also captures the enemy chief's bow, arrows and quiver. This daring episode takes pride of place in the center of the robe.

This trimmed, particularly soft tanned and painted buffalo hide shows a number of actions against the enemy, and may date from as early as 1820. It also depicts the meanderings of a bear, whose trail is marked by the dotted lines across the hide. Such renderings are unusual and are rarely shown on war history robes. It is therefore highly probable that the main human figure carrying the pipe, and thus identified as the leader of the exploits shown, has "bear power." Such power was sought by aspiring warriors, since the great strength, courage and tenacity of the bear – particularly the grizzly – was greatly admired. Note that the shield shown on pages 40–41 also seems to refer to the acquisition of bear power, which could be acquired in visions or dreams of the animal, or by purchase, generally at considerable expense, from another (see also pages 62–63).

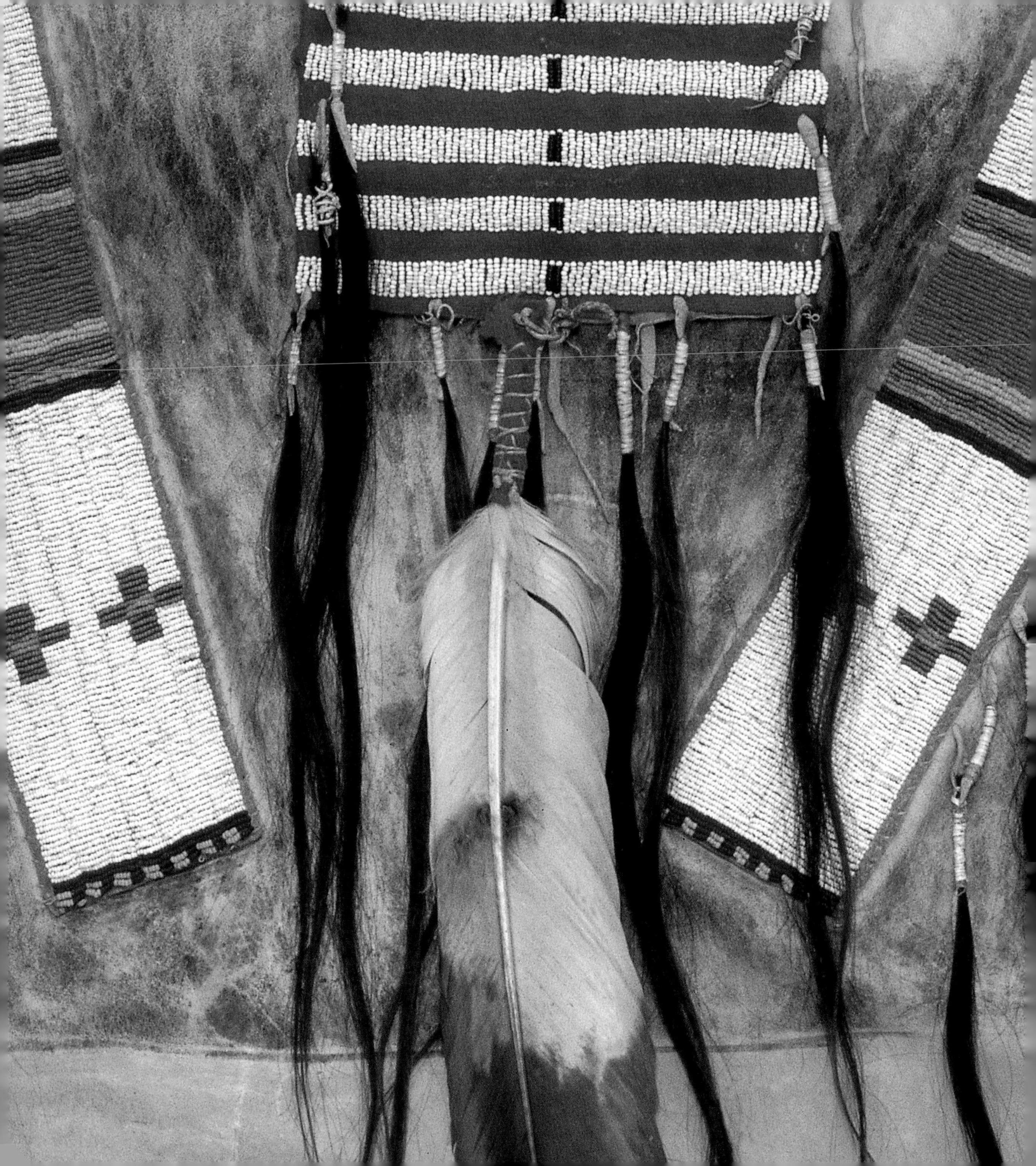

A magnificent beaded shirt worn by the prominent Miniconjou Sioux religious leader, Kicking Bear, when he visited Washington in 1896. (See Introduction, page 6.) Fabricated from two deer or antelope skins, such garments were among the most forceful of the visual statements of the Plains Indian, designating an individual of high military or social status. A distinguishing feature of these shirts was the hair-lock fringes, which were said to represent the people of the tribe for whom the shirt-wearers, the *ongloge un*, were responsible. The blue paint is symbolic of the god *Skan*; the beaded bands across the shoulders and down the arms are an elaboration of the basic hair-fringed garment, and were generally associated with the *wicasa itancans*, "leaders of men," mature individuals who combined high warrior status with the role of an influential diplomat.

Hair-fringed Shirt

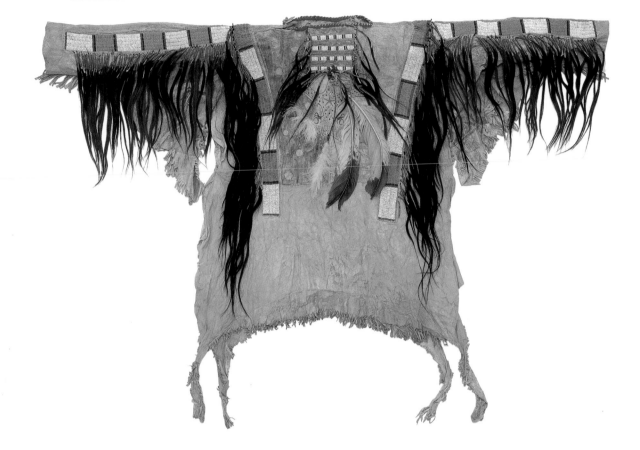

Although identified in the Smithsonian Institution records as Crow, this is atypical for that tribe and it is probably of Arapaho or Cheyenne origin, dating from circa 1880. The beaded bands are worked in the so-called lazy stitch, the seed beads sewn in lanes approximately ½ inch (1.25cm) wide. The human hair fringes are bound at their point of attachment with porcupine quills dyed red – a commonly used technique. This is a view of the back, on which is painted a Thunderbird design, adjacent to which are attached two immature golden eagle feathers. The painting and eagle feathers imply that the owner's supernatural guardian was associated with the Thunderbird, a suggestion that is reinforced by an eagle-bone whistle attached to the front of the shirt. When sounded, the whistle was considered to evoke communication with the thunder powers.

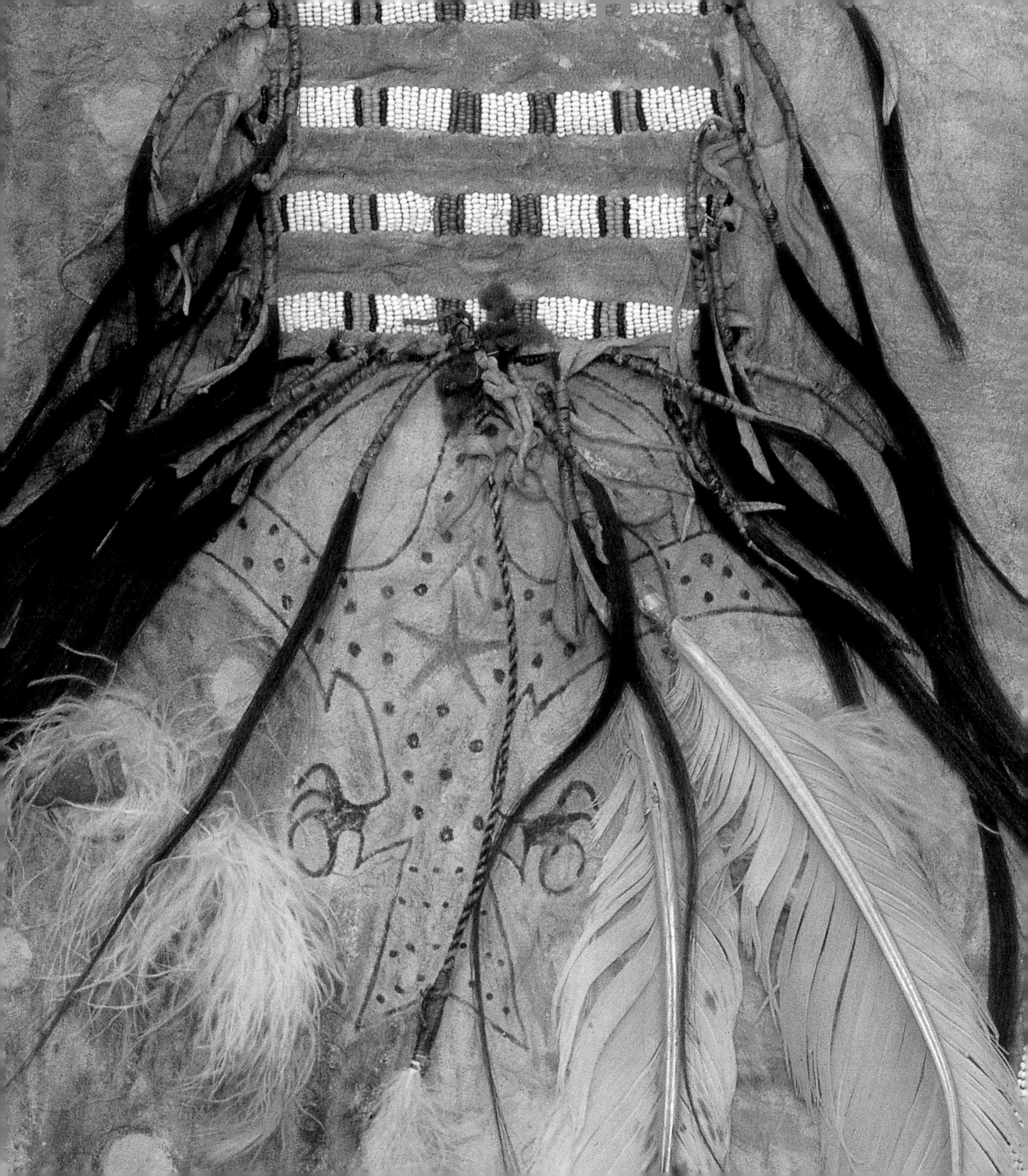

Blackfeet Shirt

This large buckskin shirt (back view) represents a specialized and early form of Blackfeet men's ceremonial regalia of the first half of the nineteenth century. Fabricated from two soft-tanned *wapiti* (elk) hides, it is embellished with bands of pony beadwork and with heavy buckskin fringes along the outer edges of each band. On the chest and back are two large panels of porcupine quillwork, a style that prevailed prior to the use of large discs (see page 118) and which, according to Maximilian Prince of Wied, an early traveler to the Plains tribes, were introduced to the Blackfeet by the Assiniboin. The design element on the panel was obviously highly symbolic to the owner and probably represented a shield or buffalo pound, but its actual meaning has gone unrecorded. This is a rare style of garment – only twelve shirts with this distinctive quilled panel are known to exist.

Crow Shirt

This very fine shirt, almost certainly Crow, dates from circa 1860. Fabricated from two antelope or black-tailed deer hides which have been beautifully soft-tanned – Crow women were renowned for their skill in skin dressing – it is embellished with bands of porcupine quillwork. The shoulder bands are worked in the so-called plaited technique, the arm bands in the quill-wrapped horsehair technique, and both are edged with blue and white pony beads. The triangular neck flap is of buckskin covered with red and green trade cloth edged with black and white pony beads and with buckskin fringes bound at their base with yellow porcupine quills. The use of discs is rather atypical on a Crow shirt. Painted designs refer to the capture of horses and weapons – lances, guns, bows, arrows – from the enemy, while the quirts signify horses bestowed as gifts.

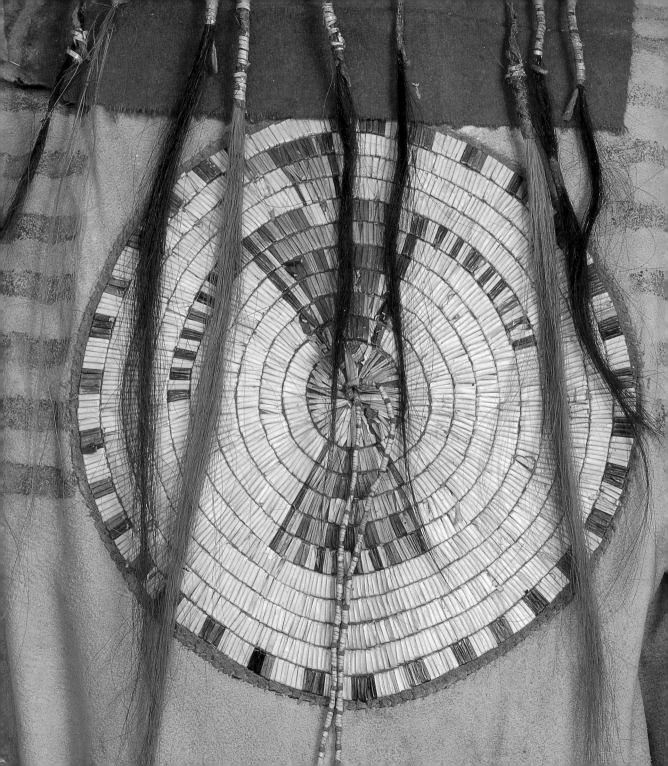

Cree Shirt

A long, beaded and quilled shirt, probably from the Cree, dating from circa 1840. Associated regalia suggests that this was formerly the property of the owner of a Medicine Pipe Bundle, one of the most powerful and sacred possessions of the Blackfeet and Cree. This is reinforced by the Thunderbird motif within the large quilled discs, which are dominant features on the front and back of the shirt. Cree and Blackfeet mythology is replete with references to the Thunderbird, and states that the flapping of its wings causes the thunder, and the flashing of its eyes, the lightning. Thunder powers were viewed as a source of both protection and courage, and most high-ranking individuals, particularly among the Northern Plains tribes, sought – through elaborate ceremonials – to acquire them, which often benefited other tribal members as well as the favored one.

Woman's dress of elk (*wapiti*) or deerskin, circa 1850. This was almost certainly collected by Lieutenant G. K. Warren after the attack on the Sioux village led by the Brulé chief, Little Thunder, which took place near Ash Hollow, Nebraska, in September 1855. Confronted by more than six hundred soldiers, Little Thunder ordered an immediate withdrawal and virtually everything was abandoned. Although this dress has been identified as Sioux, because of the circumstances under which it was obtained, it does display decided Cheyenne characteristics, not only in cut and shape but, for example, in the extensive use of black beads in the patterns. Research reveals that while the village consisted mainly of Brulé Sioux, there were some Cheyenne present. The dress could either have belonged to them, or could have been obtained through trade or intermarriage.

Sioux Robe

A magnificent painted buffalo robe dating from 1840 or earlier, in the Friedrich Kohler Collection, Berlin. Identified as the former property of a Sioux chief, it depicts various important episodes in the owner's life, not only in the theatre of warfare but also in the hunt. The heart line – considered the source of power of a living creature – is clearly rendered on the buffalo as well as on the grizzly bear (top right). This prominent warrior confronts ten enemy guns with only a bow and arrows; in another scene (top middle), with lance and shield, and wearing a U.S. military chief's coat, he overcomes a gun-carrying warrior. The rendering of the human figures, details of accoutrements, and the similarity of some of the episodes, suggest that this artist may be the same as the one who painted the fine robe now in the Smithsonian Institution (see pages 48–49).

Crow Shield

This war shield was collected by the artist Charles Schreyvogel and dates from circa 1860. It is heavy rawhide (probably buffalo) some 20 inches (50cm) in diameter, elaborately painted and embellished with clusters of chicken hawk feathers. Although not recorded at the time of collection, the visionary paintings suggest that it originally belonged to the River Crow Indian Red Woodpecker, who received instructions from a spiritual helper while on a vision quest. It documents the remarkable signs that Red Woodpecker observed, among which were clouds of hawks, a mysterious figure on horseback wearing sacred white paint, images of the moon, rain and lightning, and references to war medicine. In this way, details relating to seven shield designs were obtained by Red Woodpecker, three for home protection and four for use on the warpath.

This fine shield was collected from the Comanche by Jean Louis Berlandier in 1828. It is made of buffalo or steer rawhide some 21 inches (53cm) in diameter and ¼ inch (6.4mm) thick, and has a finely tanned buckskin cover (on the left), which is laced over the shield when not in use. Both the shield and cover are elaborately painted in a style that is typically Comanche in this period. The rawhide displays a large horned figure flanked by two monochrome human figures, one black and one yellow. Yellow is used prominently on Comanche shields, since they believed yellow gave protection to the owner. A "medicine" token, a *pouhahante* to the Comanche, consisting of four flicker feathers, is attached to the center of the black circle for protection. Seventy-three pelican feathers attached to a border of red cloth fringe the shield.

Central Plains Robe

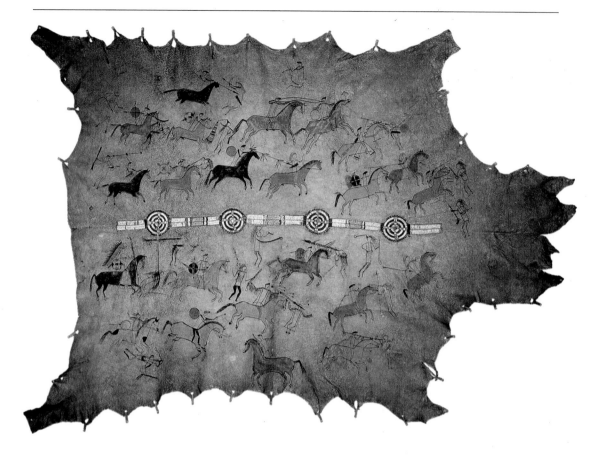

This fine painted robe was collected in 1843 by Bernus du Fay from an American Fur Company agent near the Red River while en route to Winnipeg. It is almost certainly from the Central Plains region, and recent detailed analysis of the pictographs (for example, the distinctive hairstyles of the main figures) suggests that it may be of Cheyenne origin. These main figures, with lance, bow and war axe, are causing havoc among their enemies, at least three of whom appear to be Pawnee – identifiable by the distinctive flaring cuff moccasins and pig-tail hair-style (the prostrate figure lower left). Shield designs, fringed shirts, weaponry, horse bridle styles, quirts, elaborate lances and a no-retreat sash are all depicted in these dramatic, detailed pictographs, which, in several respects, resemble those on a painted shirt now in the Musée de l'Homme, Paris.

Hidatsa Robe

Pictographic buffalo robe of *Péhriska-Rúhpa*, or Two Ravens, a distinguished Hidatsa warrior who lived permanently in the Mandan village on the Missouri River and was a friend of the well-known *Mato-tope*, or Four Bears, second chief of the tribe. The robe was a gift to the distinguished German scientist Maximilian, who resided at the village in the winter of 1834. It dramatically depicts the various war exploits of *Péhriska-Rúhpa*, who is identified by his distinctive shield bearing four painted discs and by his yellow and black painted horse. Note the way the horse hoofs are shown, a relatively common technique used by the Plains tribes at this period, which draws attention to the distinctive hoof print of an animal that transformed their society from pedestrian to equestrian nomads. The buffalo robe has been cut lengthwise for ease of tanning, then resewn.

Sarcee Moccasins

Hard-soled moccasins dating from circa 1890. The uppers are of buckskin with some yellow paint, high ankle flaps decorated with red trade cloth, and an undecorated buckskin tongue typical of this moccasin style. The tongue is bound into the moccasin, with the long buckskin thongs holding the flaps around the calf of the wearer's lower leg. The Sarcee were an Athapascan tribe associated for many years with the Blackfeet. The floral designs worked in yellow, green and red seed beads on these moccasins have been popular since about 1870, and, while there was considerable variation in pattern, there was some bias towards bilateral symmetry on the long axis – as on this pair. The uppers are sewn to the rawhide sole with heavy sinew thread; the beadwork, also sewn with sinew, is in the overlaid stitch style so typical of Northern Plains work.

Yanktonai Sioux Leggings

These fine leggings, each made of a complete pronghorn antelope skin with little trimming, were collected by Duke Paul of Württemberg when he travelled to the Missouri River tribes in the 1820s. Such a garment would have been worn by an individual of high rank who had led successful forays against the enemy. The human hair fringe documents deeds – the coups – performed by the owner and the men he led, while the inter-spersed horsehair fringes probably refer to horses captured, many of which were subsequently given away to less successful families, since generosity was an important trait of the Plains Indian. The quilled bands on the leggings are in an unusual color; frequently, the blue/green was used to dye bird, rather than porcupine, quills, although on these leggings it does seem that porcupine quills have been used.

Crow Shield

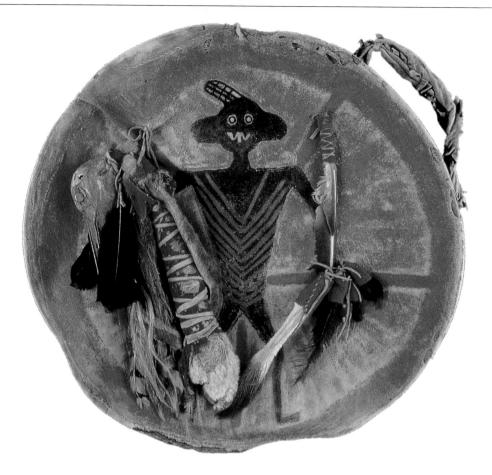

A magnificent shield of buffalo rawhide which belonged to *Arapoosh*, or Rotten Belly, head chief of the River Crow. Shown here is the buckskin inner cover, which depicts the culture hero Spring Boy at the moment when – in Crow mythology – he destroys the enemy, bringing salvation and triumph to the tribe. Attached to the shield is the head of a sandhill crane; black raven, striped hawk and golden eagle feathers, otter fur and the tail of a black-tailed deer wrapped with red wool. Recent research suggests that many Crow shield designs were derived from astronomical observation, either by the naked eye or by the use of telescopes obtained from traders. The Rotten Belly shield design appears to be inspired by a crater on the moon (referred to as "Tycho" by astronomers), above which can be discerned a triangular figure with large ears and staring eyes.

Cheyenne Horse Mask

This Cheyenne horse mask, which was collected by the scholar George Bird Grinnell, dates from 1860. It is made of buckskin, which has been covered with porcupine quillwork, fringed with cut eagle and hawk feathers, with red trade cloth, brass buttons and beads along the lower edge. During the reservation period, and even today, such masks were and are used in social gatherings and parades, enhancing the appearance and status of both rider and horse. It is possible that the idea was influenced by Spanish horse armour – certainly horse masks were in early use by the Cheyenne. The explorer Alexander Henry, who met a party of Cheyenne in 1806, recounted that some of their horses were "masked in a very singular manner, to imitate the head of a buffalo, red deer, or cabbrie with horns, the mouth and nostrils – even the eyes – trimmed with red cloth".

This case was collected in 1894 by Captain Charles E. Bendire and is thought to date from about 1880. It is made from two pieces of rawhide cut into a form resembling that of a spade, with a handle which has been sewn together with a buckskin thong and edged with red flannel. The narrow portion is decorated with tall triangles and transverse bars produced by scraping away the dark surface of the hide with a sharp knife.

Further embellishment consists of two pendants of buckskin covered with red cloth and heavily beaded; the spade shape at the bottom is similarly decorated. This interesting specimen appears to be of Crow origin and is exclusive to that tribe, who put emphasis on the sacred nature of such objects, which were associated with shields and medicine bags and were carried in parades by the wives of successful warriors.

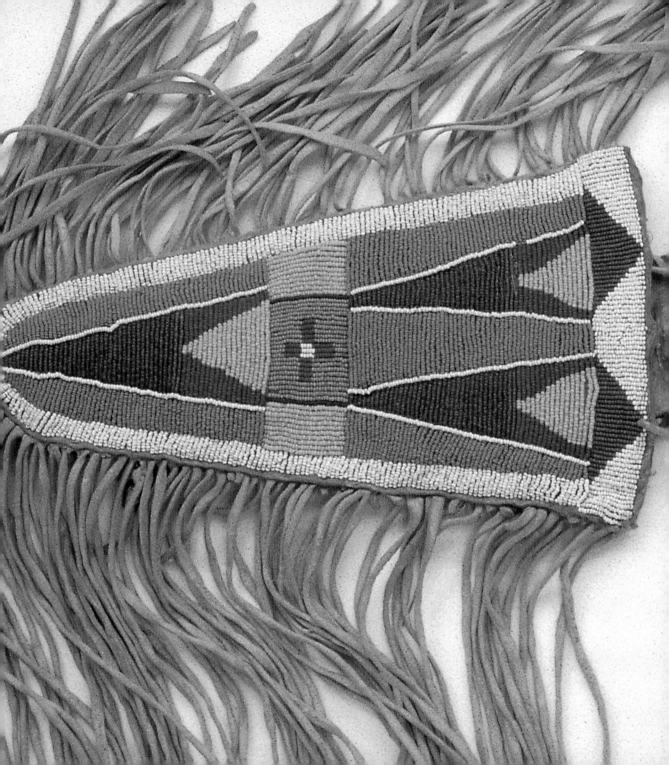

These fine leggings, dating from circa 1880, illustrate the important artistic link that existed between the Plains tribes such as the Kiowa and Comanche and the eastern bands of Apache such as the Jicarilla, Mescalero and Lipan, whose ancestors were the original inhabitants of the Southern Plains prior to their displacement by the Kiowa and Comanche. One band is sometimes referred to as Plains Apache because their original territory in the historic period ranged into what is now southeastern Colorado and northern New Mexico, which merged into the Plains region. This group produced superb buckskin clothing influenced by the costume of the Comanche, Kiowa and Southern Ute, but with a decided baroque leaning, which tends to make their work unique. These beaded leggings are boldly decorated with twisted buckskin fringes and elaborate cut flaps.

Crow, possibly Hidatsa, Crupper

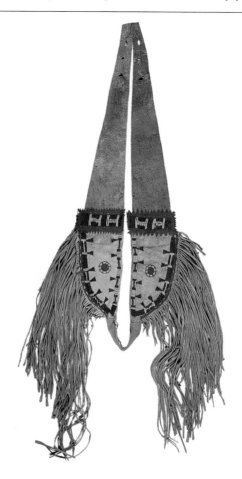

Dating from circa 1830–35, this fine crupper is made of heavy hide, probably buffalo, and soft-tanned buckskin. It is elegantly embellished with a combination of blue and white pony beads and edged with a red trade cloth with long buckskin fringe on the lower outer edges. The geometrical patterns in the beadwork were widely used on the Central and Northern Plains; however, the small triangular design elements were much favored by the Crow and Hidatsa. The blue beads were highly sought after and were first obtained through a complex trade network from the Spanish settlements in the southwest – later they were of Italian manufacture. Much basic horsegear used by the Plains tribes was undoubtedly introduced by the Spaniards; however, as with this example, the final product was generally distinctively Indian.

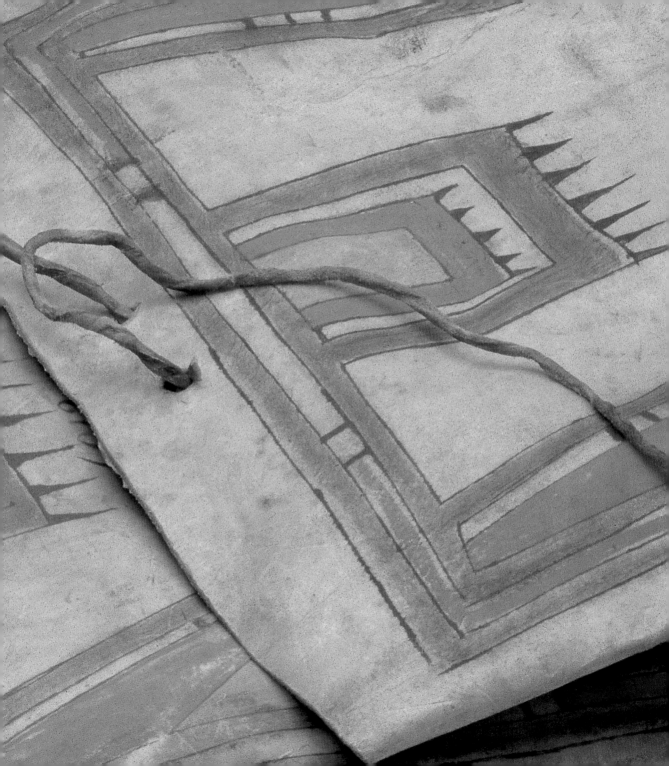

Cheyenne Parfleche

These containers were used to hold food or clothing and were made of large sheets of rawhide cut so that the shape roughly resembled that of an open envelope, which was then folded to produce the container. The term "parfleche" derives from the French description of rawhide shields, which was then extended to any article made of rawhide. In shape and size this is typical of many of the parfleches used by the Plains tribes. The careful finish, however, with a weak glue to give it a permanent sheen, and the painted geometric designs – in green, rose-red and yellow, with the patterns outlined in brown – are typically Cheyenne. It is of a style that prevailed among the Cheyenne from the early years of the nineteenth century, mainly because rawhide craft was organized by a society of women who directed the work, maintaining traditional methods and styles.

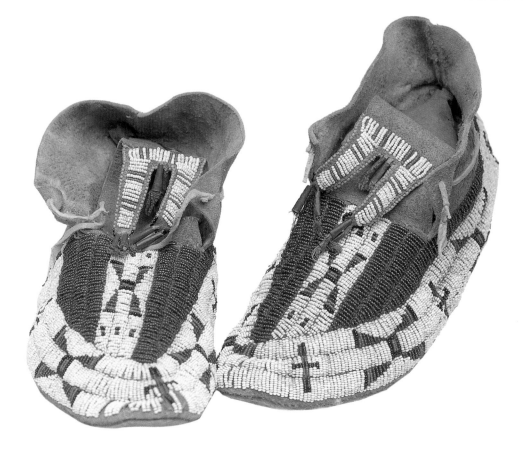

Typical Plains moccasins of the second half of the nineteenth century consisted of a rawhide sole with an upper of soft-tanned skin. The most durable were of buffalo hide sewn with sinew thread, like this pair, which dates from about 1880. The beadwork style of narrow lanes in the so-called lazy stitch characterizes these moccasins as from the Central Plains. However, the decorative elements within the beadwork and the use of black beads suggest that they may be of Northern Sioux origin, probably Hunkpapa, a band to which the famous Sioux leader Sitting Bull belonged. Note the distinctive cut of the tongue, which consists of two long, triangular skin elements tastefully decorated with seed beads on both the surface and edges, with additional embellishments of tin cone jingles to add the rhythm of sound to that of motion.

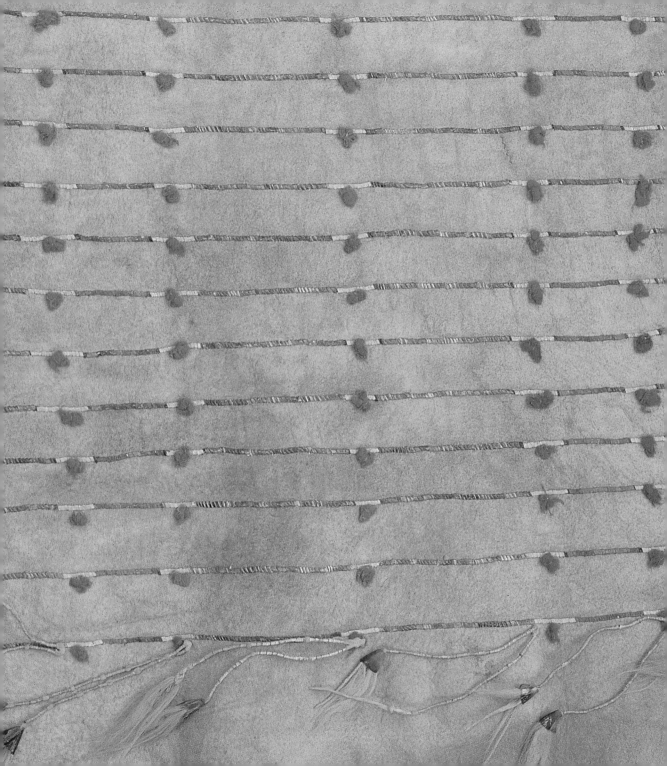

Lakota Girl's Robe

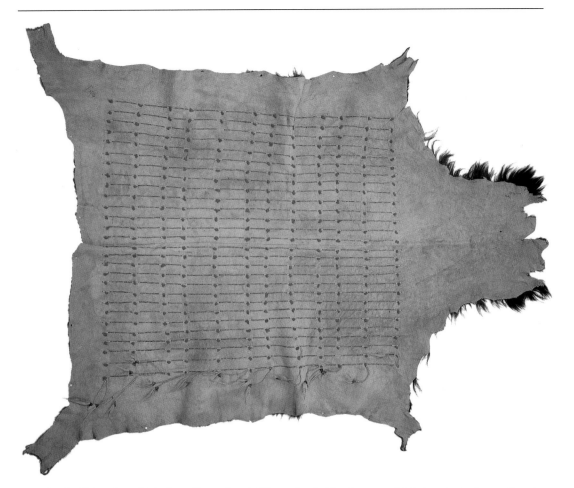

This fine buffalo robe which dates from circa 1855 is nearly 8 feet (2.4m) long and has been cut lengthwise along its middle into two pieces for tanning, then sewn back together with sinew. It is beautifully decorated with some twenty-eight narrow lanes of single-quill, double-thread porcupine quillwork in black, orange and natural white, interspersed with twelve tufts of red wool. Along the bottom of the hide are a dozen quill-wrapped buckskin thongs, which terminate in small antelope or deer hoof tips. While this is a style found on both the Central and Northern Plains, the mode of decoration had particular significance to the Sioux. It was associated with the sexual maturity of a young woman, and the quilled lines represented the trail she would travel in her mature years. For this reason, such coverings were generally referred to as "puberty robes."

Brulé Sioux Dress

This dress formerly belonged to a Sioux girl, Rosa White Thunder, who attended Carlisle Indian School in the 1880s and who sold it to the school superintendent, Captain R. H. Pratt, for $40. It is made of dark blue trade cloth with white selvedge on the sleeves, and the cut edges are bound with red and orange braid. The most distinctive decoration consists of some four hundred elk teeth attached across the upper part of the dress. This style probably originated among the Crow, since the heartland of traditional Crow territory – the Yellowstone valley in present-day Montana – abounded with wildlife, and elk were especially numerous. The teeth were rare – only the two lower incisor milk teeth of the elk were considered suitable – and since elk were not killed in great numbers by any one hunter, it was a costly business to collect sufficient teeth for a dress.

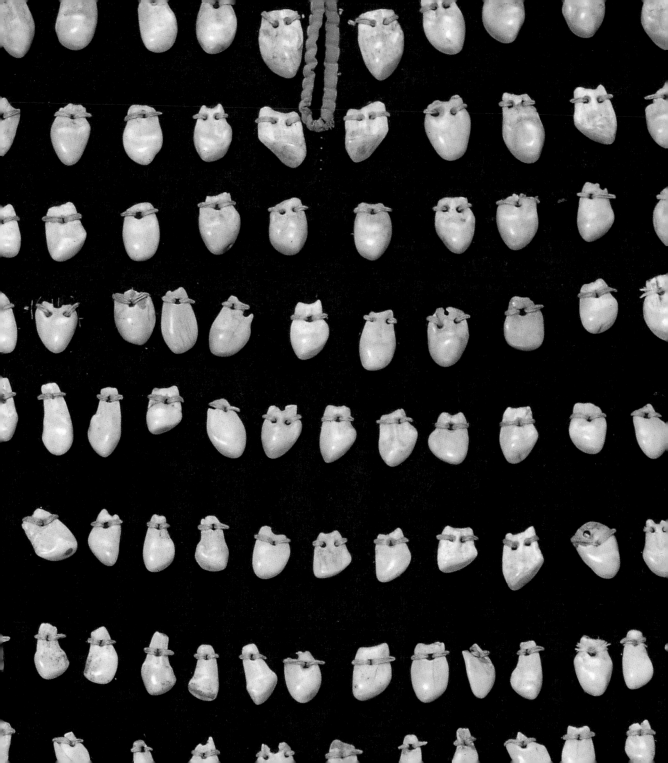

Lakota Bag

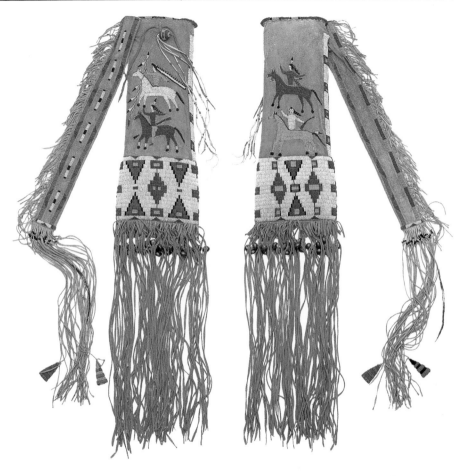

This beautifully beaded and fringed pipe-bag was collected by Major John Bourke, who was active in the campaigns against the Sioux in the 1870s. It is some 3 feet (1m) in length, and the beaded motifs, which are both geometric and realistic, are sewn with sinew thread mainly in the so-called lazy stitch. An unusual feature is the attached long sheath of buckskin, which is heavily fringed at one edge and at the bottom, where brass trade beads are threaded. This was for carrying the long pipe-stem, and the head of the pipe – probably of red catlinite, a popular material for Sioux pipes – was put into the bag itself. Many Sioux pipe-bags of this style have a further decoration at the bottom, consisting of strips of rawhide wrapped with porcupine quillwork; here, instead, are attached brass bells, the sound of which added to the attractiveness of the bag.

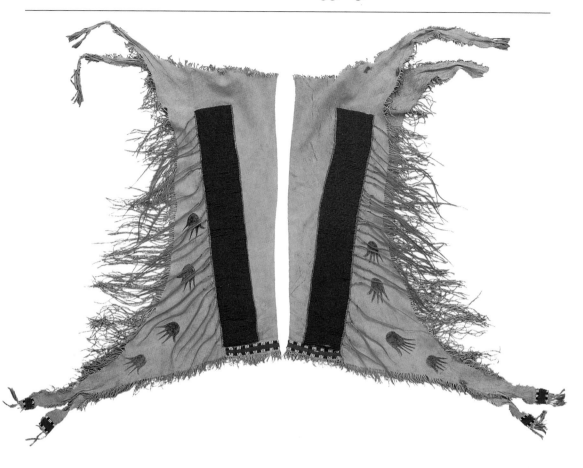

Collected in a Brulé Sioux village in 1855, these fine man's leggings exhibit a masterful combination of limited colors and natural materials, which particularly characterize ceremonial costume for this period, when trade goods were increasingly used by the Plains tribes. The leggings are made of two skins of the white-tailed deer, with minimum trimming so that the original contour of the skin is discernable. The blue pony-beaded strips have been made separately and sinew-sewn onto buffalo hide. A strip of red trade cloth is attached at the bottom center of each legging. Twenty-four locks of horsehair dyed yellow hang from the outer edge of the beaded bands, and the four painted hand prints form an additional decorative feature. Both embellishments undoubtedly refer to successes in warfare – horses captured and coups counted.

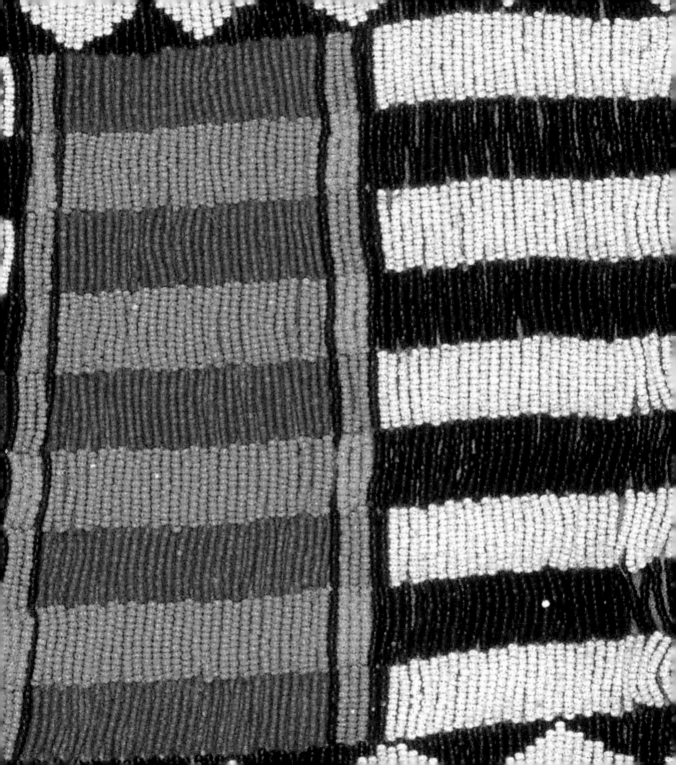

Cheyenne Leggings

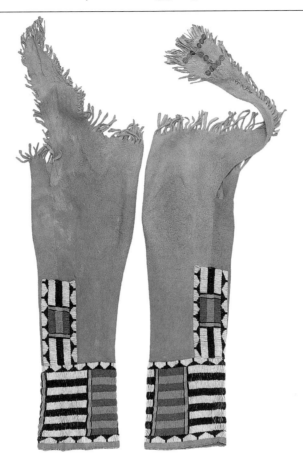

These leggings of finely tanned buckskin stained with yellow earth paint and heavily beaded, were collected in the late nineteenth century by the ethnologist James Mooney. Structurally, they conform to a style widely used on the Central Plains by such tribes as the Arapaho, Cheyenne and Sioux. They were held in place with a tie above the calf of the leg and frequently embellished with a broad band of beadwork at the bottom and a narrower band up the side. These leggings, however, are distinctively Cheyenne. Their work in this period is characterized by combinations of stripes within the pattern, generally worked with very small and carefully selected seed beads. Dark and light blue, red and a few yellow on a white background, as shown here, were favored. Some partially faceted beads, referred to as "cut beads," were also often used in Cheyenne beadwork.

Comanche Pouch

This pouch was collected by the Swiss-trained botanist Jean Louis Berlandier, who lived in Comanche country between 1828 and 1851. Made of thick, soft-tanned buckskin stained with a reddish brown earth paint, it is 3 inches (8cm) in length and 2¾ inches (7.5cm) at its greatest width across the bottom. It probably served a woman as a container for small toilet articles and was attached to the belt by two twisted buckskin cords. The pouch is elaborately decorated with metal cones and small seed beads, the designs on the flap comprising a small rosette with four projecting triangles and a border band of triangles. Artifacts from the Comanche are rare, particularly for this period. Of significant interest is the use of seed beads – they hardly made their appearance on the Central and Northern Plains until some fifteen or twenty years later.

This sash was collected in the camp of Sharp Nose, a Northern Arapaho chief who had a distinguished reputation for great bravery, sound judgement and coolness under enemy fire. Such attributes would serve a man well if he wore a no retreat sash on the battlefield, for he was expected to pin the free end to the ground and there make a stand in the face of the enemy. This particular sash is made of buckskin with a slit near the upper end, through which the wearer's head passed, and is of sufficient length to trail along the ground behind the wearer. It is embellished with five discs of quillwork; at the edges and top are decorative strips of rawhide wrapped with quills. Seven feathers from the immature golden eagle – white with brown tips – are attached to the sash, each carefully decorated with porcupine quills or beads at the point of attachment.

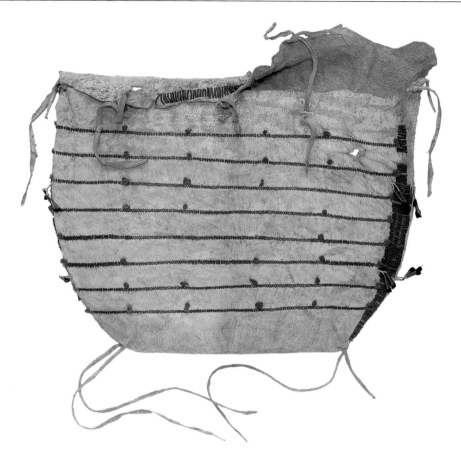

Structurally, this bag, collected in the 1850s, is typical of a style used by the Sioux well into the twentieth century. Such containers – often referred to as "tipi bags," as they were used for storage – were originally decorated with narrow lanes of quillwork across the body of the bag and broader bands at the ends, in a highly symbolic mode of decoration (see pages 90–91). This bag shows a style in transition where the eight lanes are now worked in blue and red "underwhite" pony beads and, instead of the traditional interspersed tufts of wool, there are small pieces of red trade cloth tied around the middle and then sewn in place with sinew thread. The bag is closed by an irregularly cut buckskin flap and secured by three buckskin tie thongs. There are further long tie straps at the corners of the bag for fixing to the tipi poles or the saddle during transportation.

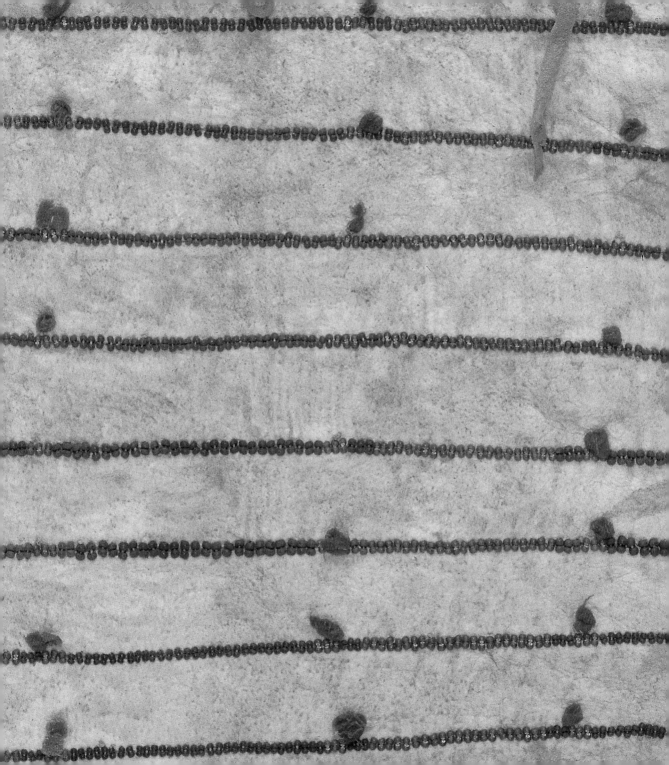

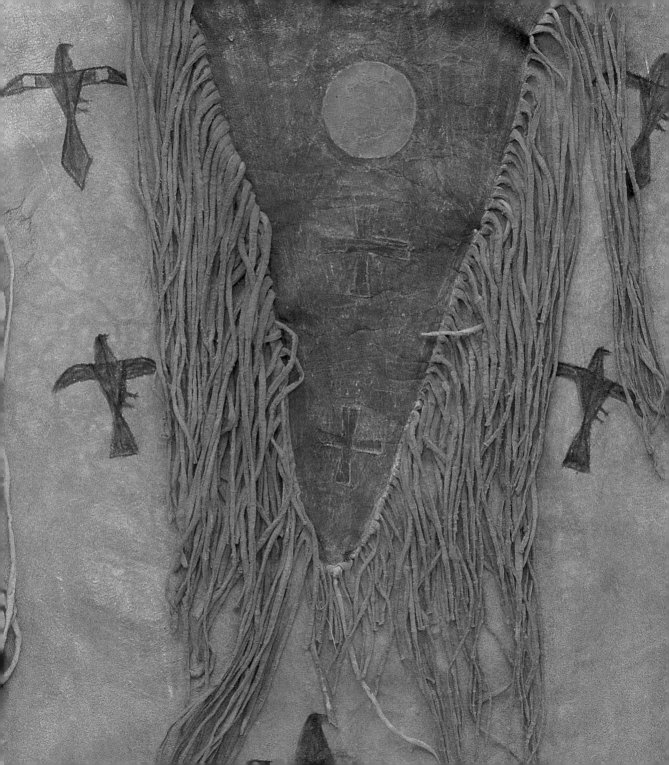

Arapaho Ghost Dance Shirt

This garment was collected in the 1890s by the ethnologist James Mooney, who made a special study of the Ghost Dance religion among several Plains tribes. In contrast to those of the Sioux, which were generally of painted muslin, this shirt is of soft-tanned buckskin. It is sinew-sewn in keeping with the Ghost Dance teachings that all garments should reflect ancient traditions of manufacture. The paintings are replete with symbolism, reflecting not only Arapaho religious teachings and mythology, but also that of the Paiute of the Great Basin, among whom – through prophet *Wovoka*'s vision during an eclipse of the sun – the Ghost Dance originated. Thus, the buffalo painted on the shoulders can be linked to appeals for resurrection of an animal vital to the lifestyle of the Plains tribes, and the magpie and sun were revered by the Paiute.

This elaborately embellished shirt, which is made of two bighorn skins, is a good example of a style used on the Northern Plains prior to about 1850. A distinguishing feature of such garments is the large rectangular quilled panel on both the chest and back. This particular shirt, accessioned as "Blackfeet," was purchased for a bottle of *eau de vie* by the French explorer Count A. F. d'Otrante when he travelled to Fort McKenzie on the upper Missouri in 1843. The body of the shirt, heavily fringed with human hair, is painted a dark brown to black, which causes the quillworked shoulder bands and rectangular panels to stand out in striking contrast. Research suggests that the predominantly red and blue elements in the quillwork of the panel are a conventionalized representation of the sun, which was considered a source of power and protection by the Blackfeet.

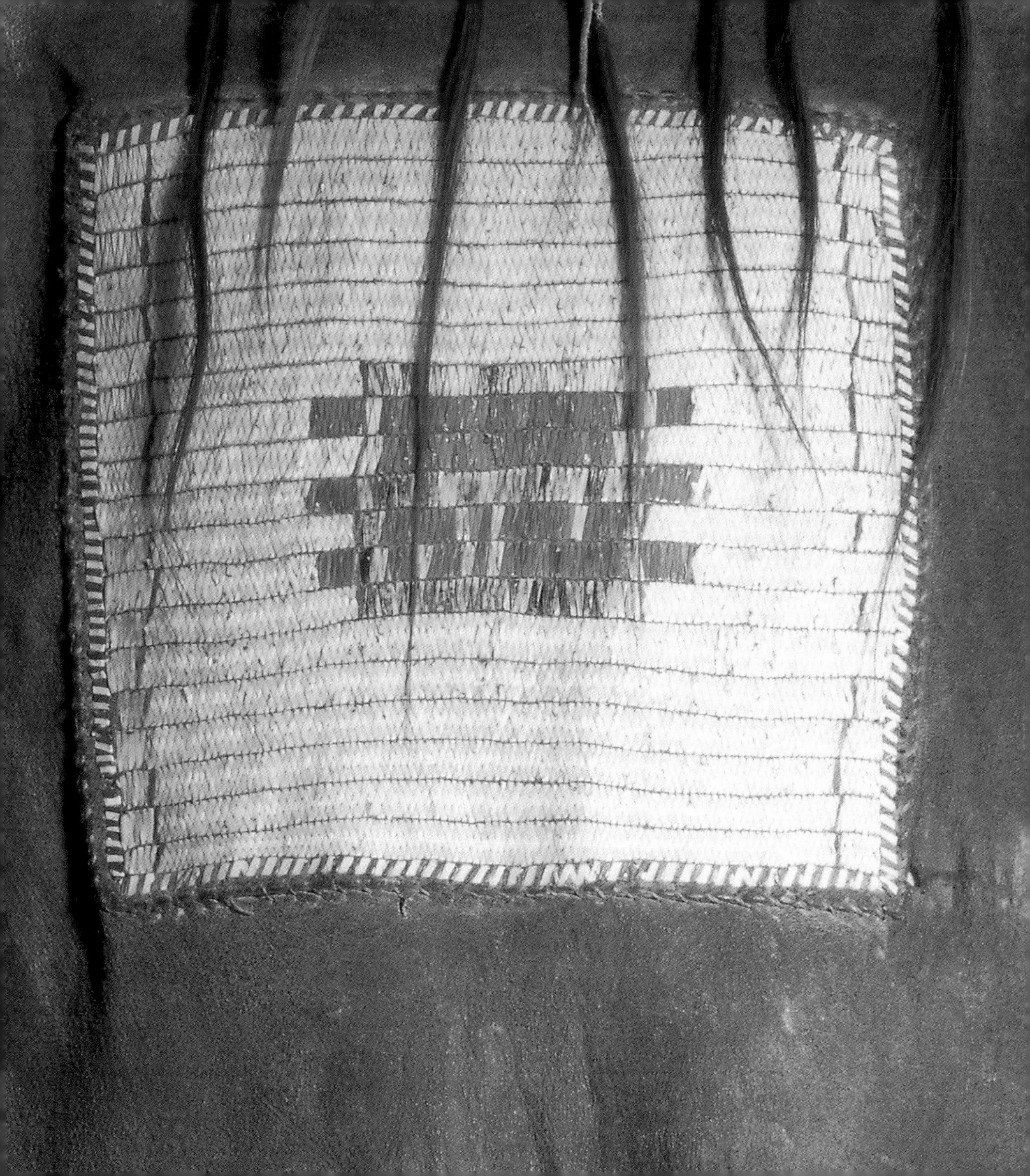

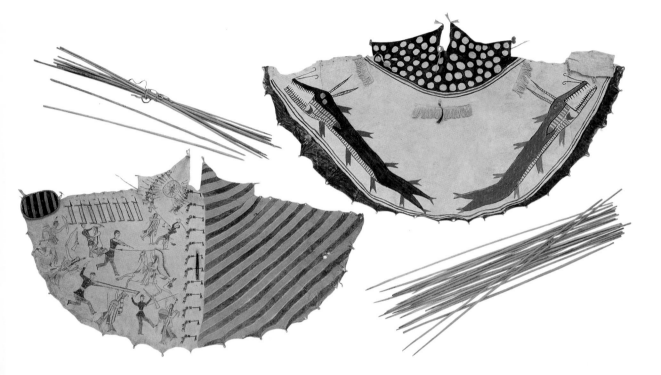

While these models date from the 1890s, and were made by Kiowa artists for the Smithsonian Institution's ethnologist, James Mooney, as part of a project on Kiowa heraldry, the designs were based on actual decorations on buffalo hide tipis of a much earlier date. Such painted tipis were owned by prominent families, and the designs were handed down through successive generations. The designs made reference to mythologi-cal figures, dreams or visions of the owner as well as war records. Thus, the design on the right probably refers to the underwater monster or horned fish – the *zemoguani* – of Kiowa mythology. That shown on the left was one of the best known and most admired Kiowa tipis as a partial record of tribal military history; the design belonged to the Kiowa head chief, Little Bluff, and was referred to as the "Tipi with Battle Pictures."

Crow Moccasins

Dating from about 1850, these moccasins are made from heavy soft-tanned hide – probably *wapiti* – in the one-piece pattern where the hide, cut to the shape of the foot, is folded lengthwise to form the upper and sole, and then sewn along one side. The uppers are tastefully embellished with a combination of porcupine quillwork and blue seed beads, the quillwork consisting of pale yellow quills as a background, with the pattern worked in orange quills and brown vegetable fiber strips. The checker weave technique used on the main panel limits the range of patterns that can be produced, and is built up of small squares in different colors. While structurally these moccasins conform to the typical Plains type for this period, the method of embellishment – quill technique, colors and types of beads used – suggests that they are of Crow origin.

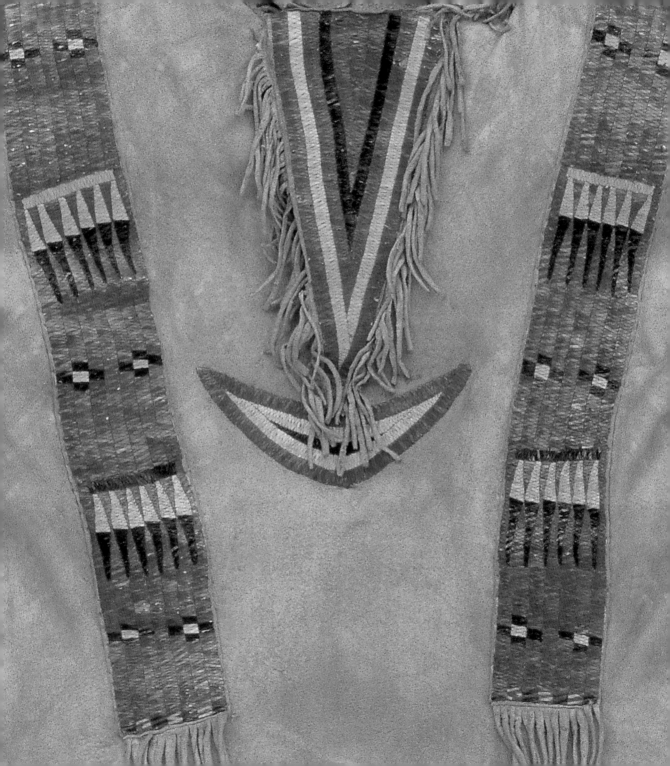

Sioux Shirt

Made from heavy soft-tanned buckskin, this beautifully quilled and fringed shirt dates from the late nineteenth century, when the skins for clothing were cut, trimmed and sewn, replacing the earlier styles which gave free play to the contours of the original hide (see, for example, pages 28–29 and 50–51). There is, however, much here that is traditional, such as the broad quilled bands across the shoulders and down the arms, worked in the complex three-quill double diamond, two-thread technique. Patterns are feather and Morning Star-type motifs, while the hands worked at the top of the arm bands almost certainly refer to a deed of valor, such as touching an enemy or capturing horses. Note that the back of the hands are shown, and both left and right hands have been carefully rendered. The neck flap is a conventionalization of a knife and sheath.

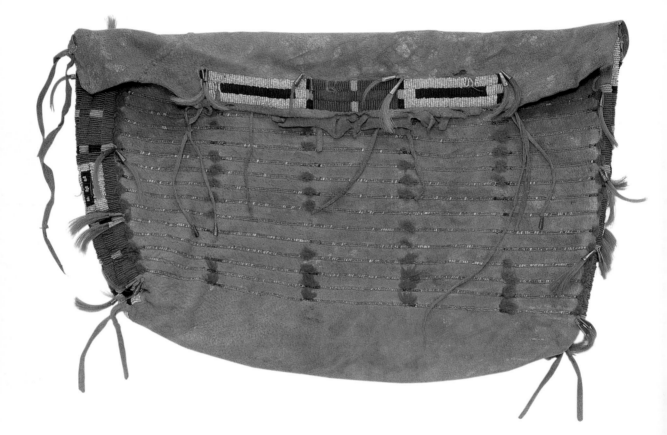

In style, this is similar to the bag shown on pages 104–105; the mode of decoration, however, differs considerably. Embellished with quillwork and panels of seed beadwork, the bag probably dates from the last quarter of the nineteenth century. It is made of soft buckskin and measures about 36 inches (lm) in length. According to Clark Wissler, an early student of Sioux decorative art, the lines or stripes of quillwork, which are predominately red, were commonly found on articles used and worn by women, and symbolically referred to the child-bearing life span of the owner, which was described as "the trail on which [a] woman travels." The ends and flap of the bag are decorated with bunches of horsehair, which have been inserted into small iron or tin cones at the point of attachment – a decorative feature highly favored by many Plains tribes.

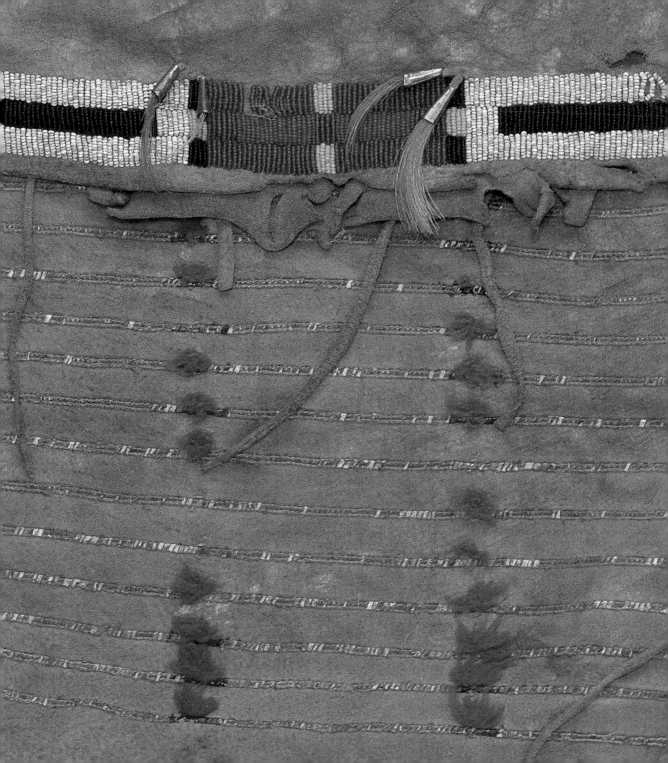

This ceremonial shirt is made from two large skins embellished on the shoulders and arms with blue and white pony beads. At the neck, front and back, are rectangular flaps of red trade cloth and hung with locks of human hair. Similar hair-locks fringe the outer edges of the beaded bands. The upper part of the body and the sleeves are painted dark brown with a red-ochre border, and sewn to the chest and back of the shirt are large discs of porcupine quillwork with patterns in orange, dark brown and blue. A large bear claw is attached to the right shoulder. This shirt would be worn by a high-ranking man successful in war and ceremonial. The pattern in the quilled disc probably refers to the Morning Star, described as the son of the Moon and Sun, and a symbol of protection. The red ochre stain suggests the shirt was believed to be imbued with "sun power."

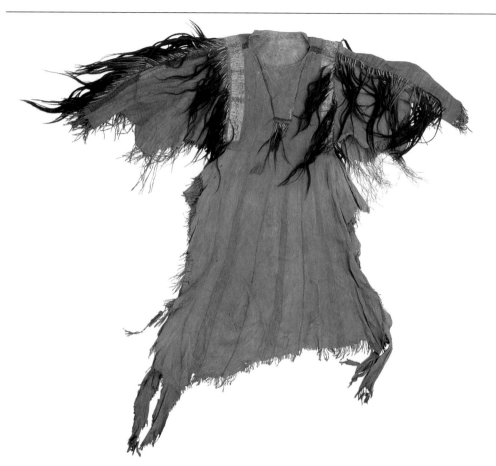

This magnificent garment, heavily fringed with black human hair and probably made considerably earlier than its date of acquisition (1874), represents a style worn by high-ranking Sioux warriors – so-called "Shirt Wearers" – who were the official executives of the tribe. At their investiture, they were presented with elaborate shirts of this type, some of which were painted with vertical black stripes, as here. One of the most important features of these "robes of office" were the hair-lock fringes, which allegedly represented the people of the tribe for whom the Shirt Wearers were responsible. Nearly 4 feet (1.2m) in length, the shirt is decorated with broad bands of quillwork over the shoulders and two lanes of blue pony beads down the arms. In keeping with early pedestrian traditions, the shirt is carefully laced together at the lower arms but open at the sides.

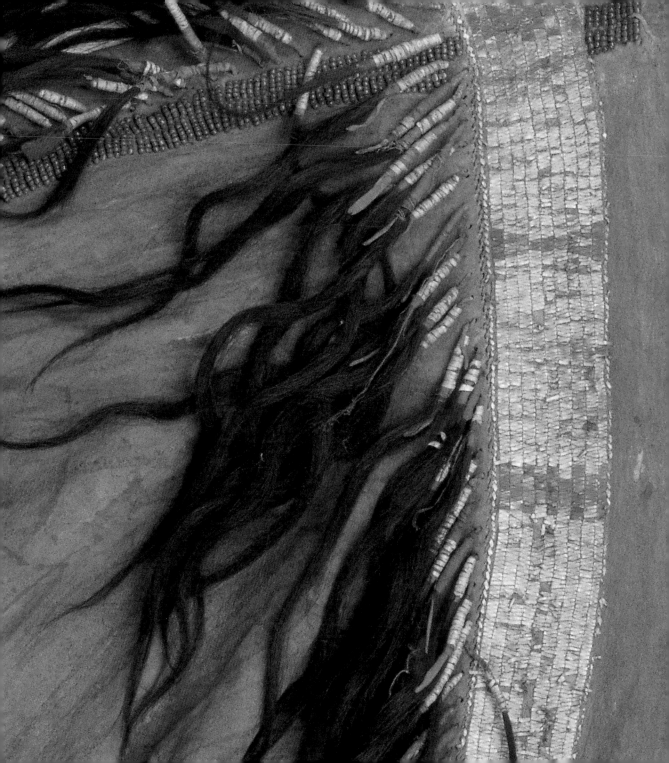

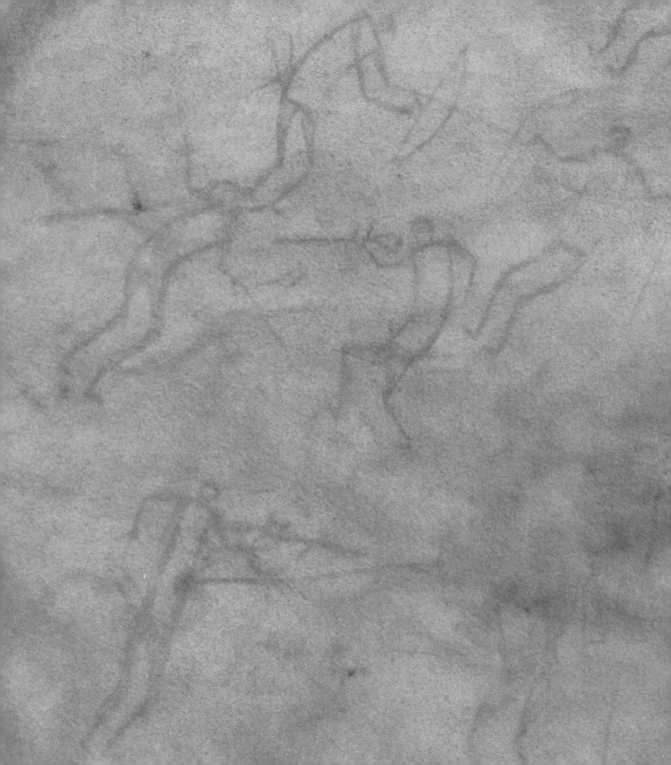

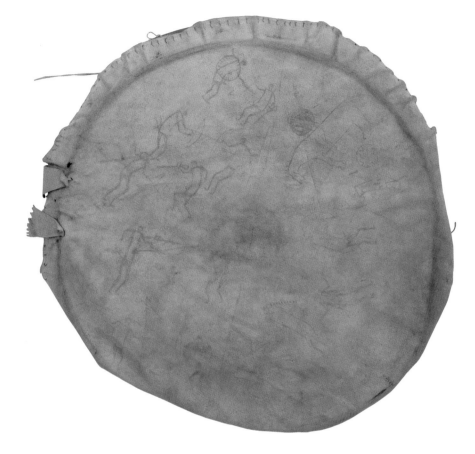

Plains shields were made of hide from the neck of a buffalo, where the skin was thickest. Early shields of the type carried by pedestrian warriors could be up to 24 inches (60cm) in diameter, and generally, as in this specimen, which was made in the early nineteenth century, had elaborately painted buckskin covers. While the shield gave mechanical protection from the enemy's weapons, it was the supernatural powers associated with it that were considered to be of prime importance. Such powers were believed to emanate from attached amulets and the appointed motifs, which were generally validated in consultation with a trusted and respected tribal medicine man. The paintings on this cover document battles between the shield's owner and his tribal enemies, probably the Sioux, who were the traditional enemies of the Pawnee.

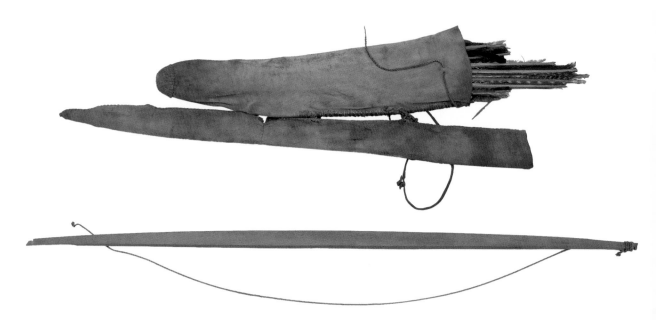

Dating from the first half of the nineteenth century, this bowcase-quiver is of heavy buckskin and has a rod sewn along the edge to facilitate easy movement of both arrows and bow. The bow, which is of the usual "flat bow" style, is 4 feet (1.2m) in length, has a twisted sinew string, and is probably made of the so-called Osage Orange wood, a highly coveted material for Plains bows. The arrows average 24 inches (40cm) in length and are fletched with hawk, wild turkey and eagle feathers. Each arrow uses three flight feathers and the shaft is painted red where they are attached. Several of the tips have long metal heads secured to the shaft with sinew thread. As with most Plains arrows of this period, the shafts have fine grooves running down their length. Symbolic of lightning, the arrows were believed to strike the same death-dealing blows as that awesome power.

This magnificent costume, formerly belonging to the Plains Saulteaux leader Louis O'soop, signals the end of an era. It was made at a time (circa 1880) when game was scarce and natural materials – buckskins, quills, ermine, sinew, feathers – were becoming increasingly difficult to obtain on the Canadian Plains. The shirt and leggings are made entirely from dark blue strouding, and the selvedge is used as a decorative feature, particularly at the top of the leggings. They are sewn with linen thread, and the horsehair locks on the shirt, dyed red, purple, yellow and green, are bound with beads at the point of attachment. The beadwork designs – stripes which probably refer to lightning, the Maltese Cross, and the Morning Star – are, however, traditional, as is the use of otter fur trim, which evokes symbolic concepts important in ancient Algonquian mythology.

Glossary & Credits

Algonquian (or **Algonkian**)
This is one of the most important linguistic families of North America, originally spoken from Eastern Canada to North Carolina and west to the Great Plains.

buffalo pound A device widely used on the Great Plains for trapping buffalo. It often consisted of a V-shaped approach to a corral into which the animals were driven.

crupper This is a strap of buckskin or rawhide fastened to the saddle and passing under the horse's tail to keep the saddle in place. It was often highly decorated by the Plains Indians.

earth paint A paint derived from a mineral source such as colored earth or rock, which was ground to a powder in small stone mortars. When used, it was mixed with water or glue.

heart line In their rendering of images of animals, the Plains tribes frequently included on them a representation of the throat and heart. The latter, together with the kidneys, was considered the source of power of the creatures.

historic period In the context of this volume, the term covers the period circa 1780-1890 which saw increasing contact with Euro-Americans and the confinement of the Plains tribes on reservations.

Indian agent Indian affairs were, and often still are, conducted through a central administrative bureau in Washington or Ottawa by local Indian agents (usually whites). The system developed to meet the demands arising from displacement of the tribes by white settlers.

lazy stitch Here the beads, strung on a sinew thread, are fastened to the surface at each end of parallel rows, $3/8$–$1/2$in (9–12mm) wide, giving a ridge-like effect. The technique was commonly used on the Central Plains.

no retreat sash These were worn by some Plains war leaders. On the battlefield, the trailing end was pinned to the ground, beyond which, custom decreed, the wearer could not retreat.

pony beads Beads of European manufacture were highly prized by the Plains tribes. In the early 1800s, small, somewhat irregular, opaque china and colored glass beads $1/8$–$3/16$in (3–4mm) in diameter were introduced by traders. They were said to have been called pony beads because they were brought in on pony pack trains. Such beads were popular until about 1850, when they were gradually replaced by the smaller seed beads. The term "underwhite" describes a pony bead – generally red – with a white core.

pronghorn antelope This animal, like the buffalo, was found in vast numbers across the Plains during the historic period. It has been described as the purest type of Plains animal, indigenous only to the Plains of North America and unrelated to the antelope family of Asia and Europe. Physically, it was something between a deer and a goat, shedding its horns like a deer, but with hollow horns like those of goats or cattle.

strouding see trade cloth.

trade cloth The nomadic Plains tribes did not practise weaving, and colored cloth obtained from white traders was highly valued. The most popular was a red or blue woollen material often referred to as strouding, because it was originally made in Stroud, England.

underwhite see pony beads.

quirt The term is derived from the description of a Spanish-American braided hide riding whip. Plains tribes modified the original style, using a wooden or horn handle with a braided hide attached.

Skan The color blue was said by the Sioux to represent one of their most powerful gods, which the shamans called Skan or To – the moving force of the universe. It was said that Skan had the most to do with the affairs of mankind.